T-Shirt

T0154377

Troth Wells joined the NI in 1972, helping to launch the *New Internationalist* magazine and build up its subscriber base. She is now the Books Editor, commissioning the *No-Nonsense Guide* and *Trigger Issues* series, and also the author of several books including the best-selling vegetarian food book *The World in Your Kitchen*; *The Bittersweet World of Chocolate* and *The World of Street Food*. Recently she has worked on a photo book published with Greenpeace, *Planet Ocean.*

NEW INTERNATIONALIST

Trigger Issues
One small item – one giant impact

Other titles in the series:

Condom

Diamonds

Football

Kalashnikov

Mosquito

About the New Internationalist

The **New Internationalist** is an independent not-for-profit publishing co-operative. Our mission is to report on issues of global justice. We publish informative current affairs and popular reference titles, complemented by world food, photography and gift books as well as calendars, diaries, maps and posters – all with a global justice world view.

If you like this **Trigger Issue** book you'll also love the **New Internationalist** magazine. Each month it takes a different subject such as Trade Justice, Nuclear Power or Iraq, exploring and explaining the issues in a concise way; the magazine is full of photos, charts and graphs as well as music, film and book reviews, country profiles, interviews and news.

To find out more about the **New Internationalist**, visit our website at: **www.newint.org**

T-SHIRT

Troth Wells

NEW INTERNATIONALIST

Trigger Issues: T-Shirt
First published in the UK in 2007 by
New Internationalist™ Publications Ltd
55 Rectory Road,
Oxford OX4 1BW, UK
www.newint.org
New Internationalist is a registered trade mark.

Series editor: Troth Wells
Design by New Internationalist Publications Ltd.

 Printed on recycled paper by TJ International, UK
who hold environmental accreditation ISO 14001.

British Library Cataloguing-in-Publication Data.
A catalogue record for this book is available from the British Library.

Library of Congress Cataloguing-in-Publication Data.
A catalogue for this book is available from the Library of Congress.

ISBN: 978-1-904456-78-0

Contents

Introduction

One of the first T-shirts I acquired, in the 1960s, was a long-sleeved maroon 'grandad' one with buttons that I found in Portobello Road market in London. I purchased some matching-colored lampshade tassel/fringe tape and sewed this onto the shirt, in true hippy style. And later in the decade I'm sure I had a black French Connection one, long before that was anything other than just a label – certainly not a 'brand' like it is now.

Anyway, T-shirts in various styles and colors were an integral part of my wardrobe. They still are. That's because they are so easy to wear, wash and manage. I'm not interested in brand-names, can't tell Dockers from Diesel, and do not want to be part of a fashion world. But whatever we wear, whether it is made of cotton, wool or leather, we are part of a global system of production involving some people who do very well out of it, and others who do not.

Cotton is popular today because it is a plant fiber and increasingly we are wanting to wear natural materials, rejecting the synthetic fabrics of acrylic, polyester and rayon. But although cotton does grow on plants, one could argue that most of it is not naturally produced: it is doused in pesticides and fertilizers; the new biotech versions are the result of highly technical gene manipulation in laboratories. In Texas, even the weather can be manipulated to produce cotton.

Today, T-shirts are the most ubiquitous cotton item, whether plain, branded, iconic or slogan-bearing; all over the world they are worn by just about everyone at some time or other, from rock stars to kids in an African village. In this way, the T-shirt is a perfect guide to the veiled world of cotton.

Troth Wells

1 What is a T-shirt?

On a trip back from the Middle East, Iraqi blogger and activist Raed Jarrar was not allowed to board a flight at JFK Airport in New York because he was wearing a T-shirt that said 'We will not be silent' in English and Arabic. Airport security forced him to change his T-shirt, saying it was like 'going into a bank with a T-shirt reading "I am a bank robber"'.

Watch out! T-shirts are powerful, make no mistake. They can strike fear into people's hearts. Who'd have thought that the real weapons of mass destruction were these soft, comfy items of clothing that just about everybody wears, as a mark of streetwise cool, fashion item or just as underwear?

But it is true that the humble cotton garment has seen a lot of front-line action over the years, from the First World War to the barricades outside meetings of the World Trade Organization today.

Where did it all begin? It seems that what we think of now as a T-shirt really began life as a vest or undergarment in the 19th century, in Europe. Some kind of undershirt had been around for centuries, but it is likely that the T-shirt evolved from a light type worn by European soldiers in World War One. The American troops, in their heavy, scratchy serge uniforms, looked on in envy. Most people think the name 'T-shirt' simply comes from the classic shape of the short-sleeved, round-necked version. Another possibility is that, because the vest was used for training, the T referred to that.

By the time of World War Two, US army and navy personnel were wearing T-shirts under their outer shirt. However it was often just worn by itself, especially for heavy, sweaty work. People began to become accustomed to this dressed-down look, and a cover of *Life* magazine in 1942 featured a soldier in his T-shirt. Cover model, even then, and the birth of the icon.

The plain vest, unencumbered by a jacket or shirt, was an obvious place to put some words. There, on the chest,

BIRTH OF A SOUVENIR

In the 1950s, options for 'wearable' souvenirs were limited, and vacationers typically brought home trinkets rather than clothing. However Quentin Sandler [of Sherry Fashions] found that one of his most popular items was a souvenir scarf, a small cotton square printed with a Floridian motif.

Today Sherry [Manufacturing Company] is one of the largest screen printers of T-shirts in the US. It remains a business focused on the tourist trade. In Key West, Florida, and Mount Denali, Alaska, and many tourist spots in between, as well as in Europe, Sherry has T-shirts for sale. Sherry's artists design motifs for each tourist market and the designs and locations are printed or embroidered on shirts in the Miami plant. ◆

Pietra Rivoli, *The Travels of a T-shirt in the Global Economy*, Wiley 2005.

for all to see the message. Who did that first? Never slow to miss a trick, it was probably the political beasts who got there ahead of the pack. Some think it was in 1948 when New York Governor Thomas E Dewey produced a 'Dew It for Dewey' T-shirt for his presidential campaign. 'I like Ike' T-shirts were worn by Dwight 'Ike' Eisenhower's supporters in 1952.

In the next few years, many of the big film stars such

as Marlon Brando, John Wayne and James Dean not only donned the garment but apparently even wore them on US TV at a time when the BBC in Britain was very much a stiff and starchy, suit-and-tie affair.

It was a small step from the T-shirt with words to the T-shirt with images and words, and here Florida was in at the start. Florida, with its pleasant climate and beaches, has long been a popular resort destination. And people like its T-shirts. As academic Pietra Rivoli says: 'Though the city fathers might prefer art galleries, it is the T-shirt

WHAT'S IN A NAME?

The sleeveless T-shirt vest is also a tank top, singlet, or 'muscle shirt' (very short sleeves) to show off male pecs. In some parts of North America and Australia and New Zealand/ Aotearoa this garment even goes by the controversial title of 'wifebeater' or simply 'beater'. The origin of the term lies in the stereotype that the shirts are worn predominantly by men who hit their wives. In the 1951 film *A Streetcar Named Desire*, the character Stanley Kowalski (played by Marlon Brando) violently rapes his sister-in-law Blanche.

shops that line the beach because that is what people want to buy.'

The types of T-shirt are wide-ranging. The ubiquitous short-sleeved one has a version called a Ringer which emerged in the 1960s. This has one plain color with the collar and ends of the sleeves in a different color. Colorful tie-dyed and screen printed garments soon followed, sixties psychedelia. Then there are long-sleeved, buttoned 'grandad' T-shirt, sleeveless tank tops or vests, V-necks and buttoned, collared ones too.

In *Raging Bull* (1980), the main character, Jake LaMotta (played by Robert de Niro), often wears a vest around the house, including in one scene where he beats his wife.

The vests have been popular in the street gang culture of North America. From there the wearing of 'wifebeaters' spread to hip-hop culture; the vests are often worn by hip-hop artists in public, on stage, or in the media. The sleeveless T-shirt is also seen as an item of punk fashion since it is generally regarded as anti-fashion because of its informal appearance. The term has been denounced by the US-based National Organization for Women (NOW), which says that it trivializes domestic violence. 'The implication is that wife-beating is not viewed as sufficiently serious to lift it above the level of something that's OK to joke about,' says the president of NOW. ◆

ROCK TEES MAKE A FASHION STATEMENT

Blame David Bowie. A Thin White Duke T-shirt propelled a little white lie, which snowballed with every wearing. Being too young to attend a show on Bowie's 1983 Serious Moonlight tour, I did what any underage doofus would do. I bought a concert T-shirt – three-quarter-length blue sleeves, image of Major Tom himself on the front. Then the untruths unfolded. (Cool older guy at school: 'You saw Bowie?' Me: 'Yeah, of course. Don't touch my shirt, man.') I was in da club (decades before you, 50 Cent). And today, every Jane and Joe Sixpack can belong – whether or not they went to the show, thanks to the appearance of concert T-shirts at stores from Bloomingdale's and Macy's to JC Penny, Kmart and Target. Many of these new threads look like they could be oldies – there are Jimi Hendrix and Beatles T-shirts galore at Target. Is this is what the fashionable call 'retro-hip'?

Howard Kramer works as the curatorial director at the Rock and Roll Hall of Fame in Cleveland. 'The first T-shirt with a rock likeness was put out by an Elvis Presley fan club around 1956,' he says. 'It's very rare and had a rendering of the famous Tampa '55 photo on it, colorized.' And me? Never did see Bowie, and I was also too young to get into the Malibu Night Club in Lido Beach when U2 played there in 1981. But when Bono and the boys – they really seemed like boys back then – came to the Nassau Coliseum for the first time on 3 April 1985, I was there. And that's the truth. ◆

Kevin Amorin, *Newsday* 17 October 2005 www.newsday.com

In the 1970s, the black T-shirt came to the fore as the essential item to wear at rock concerts, both for the performers and the audiences. Bearing the band's name and image, the T-shirts walked off the stalls at gigs and fans could wear them to the next event. Some of those rock concert classic T-shirts are collectors' items today.

We wear T-shirts with slogans or images or brands to reinforce a club or membership sentiment: we all like this band, this event, we all hate x, or disapprove of y, we are all animal lovers, or we are anti-war; we support this team, or we are cool because we know to wear this brand, or this color, or this style.

Wherever you go today, even if it is just down your town's shopping street or mall, you will probably find a T-shirt depicting the wonders of where you live, or supporting the local baseball or football team. If you are in a tourist hot-spot, the range of T-shirts is overwhelming, from green parrots in Miami to palm trees in Phuket. There are brightly-colored tsunami and Hurricane Katrina memorial T-shirts too.

The image and slogan of the T-shirt enables them to be worn like an extra facet of your personality: they are saying something for you. It could simply be that you want people to know you have been to Phuket, or that someone who has been there gave you the T-shirt. Or, if your wording is 'Save the Whales' you presumably have some interest in species preservation. There are all kinds of slogans and words and images, some explicitly political or violent, some funny and thought-provoking. Branded fashion-wear is another target, with anti-Nike slogans such as 'Don't Just Do It', 'The Swooshtika' or gay messages like 'Gender rebel' and 'It's ok, it's only love'.

But one thing T-shirts generally have in common is that they are made of cotton.

2 Cotton tale

The world's favorite fabric has a long history which stretches back thousands of years. On the way the cotton tale has encompassed fashion in India and France, Columbus's mistaken view that he had reached Asia, the wretched period of slavery in the Americas and the legacy of child slavery today – not to mention Britain's industrial revolution, the blues, Gandhi's defiance, idealism, skulduggery, hip-hop... and a tiny but persistent insect, the boll-weevil.

The plant

Gossypium – cotton – is a scrawny, unlikely plant to be the center of so much attention. The ancestor of today's varieties is a perennial swamp mallow, *G malavacae*. Originally tropical, cotton is also grown today in the US and Russia. Wild cotton seeds with their tough outer casings (bolls) floated over the seas and found homes in many places in the world. The four key species are *G hirsutum* – the most widely used, accounting for over 90 per cent of production. Then there is the long-stapled *G barbadense*, and finally *G herbaceum* and *G arboreum*. The last two have been cultivated for centuries in the Old World, with fragments of cotton cloth found in Pakistan dating back more than 5,000 years. The plant may have been grown even earlier in Arabia and Syria.

While the Indian subcontinent still mainly grows these varieties, the dominant one today comes from the Americas. In the New World, sites in Peru dating back 4,500 years have revealed cotton bolls and fiber remains of the *barbadense* variety. But the oldest remains in the region, found in Mexico, are dated 5,500 BCE, and are probably *G hirsutum*. The Spanish took the American varieties of cotton to Europe and the Portuguese conveyed them to Africa and India. Today, cotton is grown as an annual plant in three main types: Upland (*G hirsutum*), Sea Island (*G barbadense*) and Egyptian (*G barbadense*). Upland appeared in the mid-18th century in southeastern US, probably coming from the Caribbean. In 1793 Eli Whitney invented the cotton 'gin' (from 'engine') that transformed the pace of cotton production, and cultivation of Upland cotton spread across the US South to Texas. The Civil War

WORLD COTTON PRODUCTION

	2001/2	2002/3	2003/4	(Millions of 480-lb. bales) 2004/5	2005/6	2006/7
China	24.4	22.6	22.3	29.0	26.2	30.9
US	20.3	17.2	18.3	23.3	23.9	21.7
India	12.3	10.6	13.8	19.0	19.2	21.0
Pakistan	8.3	7.8	7.8	11.1	9.9	9.7
Brazil	3.5	3.9	6.0	5.9	4.7	6.0
Uzbekistan	4.9	4.6	4.1	5.2	5.6	5.4
African Franc Zone	4.5	4.1	4.4	5.0	4.2	4.4
Turkey	4.0	4.2	4.1	4.2	3.6	4.0
Australia	3.3	1.7	1.7	3.0	2.8	1.2
EU	2.6	2.2	2.0	2.3	2.5	1.6
Syria	1.7	1.1	1.3	1.6	1.5	1.1
Egypt	1.4	1.3	0.9	1.3	0.9	1.0
Turkmenistan	0.9	0.7	0.9	0.9	1.0	1.1
Tajikistan	0.7	0.7	0.8	0.8	0.6	0.6
Kazakhstan	0.6	0.5	0.6	0.7	0.7	0.7
Others	5.4	5.1	6.2	7.0	7.0	6.2
World Total	**98.8**	**88.3**	**95.1**	**120.3**	**114.1**	**116.6**

Source: USDA

WORLD COTTON CONSUMPTION

	2001/2	2002/3	2003/4	2004/5	2005/6	2006/7
				(Millions of 480-lb. bales)		
China	26.3	29.9	32.0	38.5	45.0	50.0
India	13.3	13.3	13.5	14.8	16.5	18.0
Pakistan	8.5	9.4	9.6	10.8	11.8	12.2
Turkey	6.2	6.3	6.2	7.1	6.9	7.0
US	7.7	7.3	6.2	6.7	5.9	5.0
Brazil	3.8	3.6	4.0	4.2	4.1	4.0
EU	5.3	4.8	3.8	3.4	2.7	2.3
Indonesia	2.3	2.3	2.2	2.2	2.2	2.2
Bangladesh	1.2	1.6	1.6	1.9	2.2	2.3
Thailand	1.8	2.0	1.9	2.1	2.1	2.1
Mexico	2.2	2.1	2.0	2.1	2.1	2.1
Russia	1.8	1.7	1.5	1.4	1.4	1.4
Taiwan	1.3	1.2	1.2	1.2	1.2	1.2
South Korea	1.5	1.5	1.4	1.4	1.1	1.1
Uzbekistan	1.2	1.2	1.3	0.9	0.8	0.8
Other	10.3	10.5	10.0	10.3	10.0	9.9
World Total	**94.4**	**98.5**	**98.2**	**108.8**	**115.8**	**121.3**

Source: USDA

– partly caused by the South's determination to use slaves on its cotton plantations – interrupted production and other countries began to grow the species to plug the gap.

Sea Island cotton developed in the island and coastal plains of Georgia and the Carolinas in the late 18th century, originating from a South American and Caribbean variety. It has very long, fine, high-quality 'lint' – the fluffy strands that stick to the seed and become woven into thread. It was particularly susceptible to the boll-weevil that arrived from Mexico early in the 20th century and wiped out much of US cotton production.

Egyptian cotton was originally identified in 1820 in Cairo – Jumel's cotton – but most likely came from South America via Nigeria. It was hybridized with Sea Island types.

The key difference between the types, in terms of what would become a highly commercialized industry, is the length of the hairs or 'staple'. The *hirsutum* fibers are about one inch long, while the *barbadenses* are almost double that length and are easier to work. Over the years, the New World types have become the dominant ones, the workhorses of the looms.

While it is clear that cotton production stretches back a long way, it is not so clear how somebody lighted on the idea of exploiting the scratchy cotton boll. But it is interesting that the way the plant was domesticated and converted into yarn was similar even though it occurred in different places. The use of combs, spindles and looms was always there.

Spinning and weaving were nearly always done by women in early cultures, and today it is usually women who work in the factories to create the T-shirts we wear.

The earliest cotton cloth to come to Europe came from Asia, probably from the Indian subcontinent. Ancient fragments were found at Mohenjo Daro, from cotton cultivated 5,500 years ago by the Harappans of the Indus Valley. In the Hindu texts of the *Artharva Veda* day and night are represented by two sisters weaving, one the warp and the other the weft.

India traded its cloth to China for spices and other goods. Cotton clothing was common by the time Alexander the Great swung through the region in 325 BCE – one of his soldiers described the bolls as 'nuts that produce wool'. The 'vegetable wool' became very useful for padding their saddles, and they carried the cloth back to Greece.

Before the time of the Incas in Latin America, cotton was allowed to grow in its natural state, and was yellowy brown to purplish red. Today most cotton is naturally off-white or grey before it is bleached. Cotton garments could

'I'm into cotton underwear. I don't need cheetah-print leather to make me feel sexy.'

Nelly Furtado, Portuguese-Canadian singer.

be a means of artistic expression, woven with detailed patterns often with religious or social symbolism. When the Spanish arrived in the late 15th century cotton was widely cultivated in Central America; this was the *hirsutum* that became Upland and today makes up over 90 per cent of all the cotton grown.

In Europe, cotton was a luxury item; most fabric was created from linen, hemp or wool. Arab traders saw an

---

MAKING COTTON

Compared with more manageable wool (from sheep or alpaca), and linen (from the flax plant), cotton is fiddly and difficult to work. First, the lint has to be pulled from the bolls. It is tangled, covered in bits of pod and has to be cleaned by washing. Then it must be combed to pull all the fibers smoothly in one direction, creating longer strands that can be twisted into thread using a spindle and distaff. The thread would often break and have to be twisted back together in this painstaking and delicate operation.

Next came the weaving. In earliest times, the loom was probably furnished by a low horizontal branch of a tree. The 'warp' or vertical threads would be attached to the bough and secured on the ground. Then the horizontal 'weft' was threaded through the warp, over and under, and pushed up firmly row on row to create a cloth. ◆

---

opportunity and by the 7th century BCE they were supplying cotton to Venice, the hub of Mediterranean trade.
Rather than use the Hindu name 'karpasi', the Muslim
traders called the cloth 'qutun', which became cotton. In the
medieval period, cotton was woven with wool into fustian.
In his book *Cotton* Stephen Yafa tells of the English knight
Sir John Mandeville who traveled in the 14th century to
what is now Turkey where he came across 'a remarkable
animal-plant called the Vegetable Lamb'. Mandeville ex-
plained that the cloth was 'harvested from a wool of a rare
and exotic baby sheep' in a place where lambs grew on

THE DEMISE OF INDIAN COTTON

'The story of cotton in India is not half told, how it was
systematically depressed from the earliest date that American
cotton came into competition with it about the year 1786, how
for 40 or 50 years after, one half of the crop was taken in kind
as revenue, the other half by the sovereign merchant at a price
much below the market price of the day which was habitually
kept down for the purpose, how the cotton farmer's plough
and bullocks were taxed, the *Churkha* taxed, the bow taxed and
the loom taxed; how inland custom houses were posted in and
around every village, on passing which, cotton on its way to the
Coast was stopped and like every other produce taxed afresh;
how it paid export duty both in a raw state and in every shape

shrubs. The idea of cotton as a sort of animal persisted for some time in other colorful accounts of exotic travels.

Cotton's attractions were increasing. In the 17th century the everyday cloth reinvented itself as possibly the first major fashion item to hit northern Europe – glazed Indian cotton or chintz. Vasco da Gama had reached India in 1498 and brought back both fine muslin and the ordinary calico which was often used plain and unglazed as well as glazed into chintz. When England and France cottoned on, they couldn't get enough. Colored cottons stormed the household as furnishings and later the fabrics began to be used

---

of yarn, of thread, cloth or handkerchief, in which it was possible to manufacture it; how the dyer was taxed and the dyed cloth taxed, plain in the loom, taxed a second time in the dye vats, how Indian piece goods were loaded in England with a prohibitory duty and English piece goods were imported into India at an *ad valorem* duty of 2½ per cent. It is my firm conviction that the same treatment would long since have converted any of the finest countries in Europe into wilderness. But the Sun has continued to give forth to India its vast vivifying rays, the Heavens to pour down upon the vast surface its tropical rains. These perennial gifts of the Universal Father it has not been possible to tax.' ◆

from Francis C Brown, British cotton planter in Malabar, India in 1862. www.craftrevival.org/

as underwear, replacing scratchy wool, and as summer garments. By 1664, the British East India Company was importing over 250,000 pieces of calico and chintz and the new material was edging out wool in people's wardrobes, and the trend led to uproar in the wool and silk industries.

And what was the response? Ban cotton imports! Moral high ground, xenophobia and religion were all brought into the fray: a pro-wool pamphlet talked of 'tawdry calico, a foreigner by birth, made by a parcel of heathens and pagans that worship the devil.' But government diktats were ignored as market forces held sway and people bought the brightly decorated Indian cloths. Government bans were later replaced by duties on imports but by that time the European producers had copied both Indian dye techniques and designs so they could produce the colorful cloth at home. As has happened so many times since, European development thrust thousands of Indian artisans out of work. And then came the 'logical' next step: to acquire India itself, with its cotton and its textile industry. The public-private partnership of the British Government and the East India Company gained the support of the Mughal emperors and took control in 1757. Eventually India was not allowed to produce its own cotton cloth. The cotton was instead shipped to England's dark satanic

> **INDIAN WORDS connected with cotton that have passed into the English language**
>
> | | | |
> |---|---|---|
> | Dungaree | Jodhpur | Chintz |
> | Gingham | Sash | Calico |
> | Khaki | Seersucker | |
> | Pajamas | Shawl | |

mills and then, if an Indian wanted a cotton garment they had to buy the imported English product. England's exports helped subsidize the slave trade, as the cotton was traded for slaves in West Africa. 'In a few short decades,' says Yafa, India became 'a beggar at the mercy of Her Imperial Majesty's mercantile whims'.

The problem in Europe was that demand outstripped supply of the desirable cloth. In the Age of Enlightenment, finding a solution was the challenge. New technologies were developed, and in England Richard Arkwright's mill revolutionized the cotton industry and launched the Industrial Revolution. He had come across James Hargreaves' mechanized spinning jenny (named for Hargreaves' daughter) that in 1764 boosted the output of yarn. In true entrepreneurial style, Arkwright ripped off the jenny idea, raised money and persuaded the public that cotton spinning was no longer suited to family labor at home, but rather to his factory mill in Lancashire.

Other inventions such as the flying shuttle to speed weaving helped the mechanization process, and the first Arkwright water-driven mill opened in 1771 with hundreds of workers provided with housing and chapel.

Arkwright's yarns were sent out to weavers across England, and cloth output soared, as did raw cotton imports – from 4.7 million pounds in 1771 to 56 million pounds in 1800. By now, it was not only the upper classes that could afford cotton clothes; even servant girls had gowns and stockings made of cotton.

The next requirement was a mechanized loom to has-

THE ARMANI OF HIS DAY

In the mid-18th century, style meant Christophe-Phillip Oberkampf, based at his textile factory in Versailles, Paris. Louis XV's mistress Madame de Pompadour wore Oberkampf's stunning gowns and proclaimed him an 'inspired genius'. He was cotton's first celebrity designer, a favorite also of Marie Antoinette – and later of Napoleon, who awarded him the Cross of the Légion d'Honneur in 1809, saying: 'We will make together a rude war against the English, you by your industries and I by my armies.' ◆

From Stephen Yafa, *Cotton: the biography of a revolutionary fiber*, Penguin 2005.

---

ten the manufacture of cloth. This resulted from the invention of Edmund Cartwright, a priest, who employed a carpenter and a blacksmith to translate his ideas into reality. James Watts' steam engine provided the power for the loom that was to set the seal on the factories of the new industrial age.

Not everyone was happy of course. The hand-weavers, out of work as mills spread, began to attack and destroy the factories. But in the end, the force of capitalism destroyed the artisans. The new workers included many children; some 200,000 were in Manchester's mills in 1839. Their main job was to step in and out of the looms to tend the bobbins, replacing and re-tying thread.

Meanwhile, in America

At first, America's cotton was a small crop, planted originally in the Jamestown settlement in 1607. Most cotton and cotton goods still came from Britain. Fustian – cotton woven with wool – was the usual clothing material as it was warm and robust. Sea Island cotton came in from the West Indies and took root in the Carolinas and Virginia. They exported the produce to the other colonies in New England. And while people may think that New England was always anti-slavery, in fact colonies there provided the first group of slave-traders, their Puritan religion apparently no barrier to bringing Africans across the Atlantic and selling them to the West Indies in exchange for cotton and rum. According to historian Lorenzo Johnston Greene, the slave trade was a major foundation of New England's economy, creating 'a wealthy class of slave-trading merchants, with profits going into the colony's

COTTON CONNECTIONS

Allusions to cotton and weaving pop up in many areas from songs and Greek mythology to everyday slang:

Spinning a yarn – telling a tale that is probably not true in all its details.

Cotton on – get the drift.

Stitch-up – frame someone.

Fair-to-middling – no better than average quality (from cotton classification).

Spin doctor – PR expert who makes things appear better than they are.

Threading through – negotiating an intricate, tricky route.

'Lintheads' – derogatory term for people who worked in the cotton mill.

Cotton candy – candy floss.

Cottontail – Rabbits named after their tail, which is shaped like a cottony ball.

growth and development'.

At this time, people were spinning and weaving mainly hemp and linen as cotton was less available. They used hand-tools as English mechanized looms and spinners had not yet reached these shores.

The wealthy merchants were not prepared to wait for-ever. Others were also looking to the future with cotton.

Cottonmouth – Large, aquatic, venomous snake found in wetlands, rivers and lakes. It gets the name from the defensive habit of gaping its mouth open to expose the white lining of the mouth, warning potential aggressors to stay away.

Cotton-top tamarin – A small monkey named for the crest of long, whitish hairs from the forehead to the nape and flowing over the shoulders.

Cotton Penelope – a type of canvas cloth used in needlepoint. It is named for Penelope, the wife of Odysseus in Greek mythology. While Odysseus was away for long years, Penelope was pestered by suitors. She insisted on finishing her weaving before she would consider any offers. She was busy by day, but at night she unraveled her work so that it was never completed, to keep men from claiming her. ◆

After the War of Independence against Britain in 1776, American leaders needed to prove the nation could stand on its own two feet. Self-sufficiency was the key and cotton had a part to play. The first US President, George Washington, knew a lot about cotton; he even used to weave it to make clothes. Thomas Jefferson, the third President, noted that in four Southern States, 'The poor are almost entirely clothed in [cotton] in both winter and summer'. These states were already supplying cotton to the North. And they could see that although England had industrial might, it did not have raw cotton. When the fledgling independent colonies gained a stronger federal government in 1789, cotton was on its way. But machines were needed to develop their home-grown industry.

Industrial espionage

Nicking other people's inventions was a key part of the cotton story. Arkwright disregarded patent laws, so he would not have been surprised when Samuel Slater, a former superintendent at an English mill, memorized the workings of the water frame spinning machine, and recreated it in Rhode Island. The Slater mills used cotton from the Caribbean region and produced yarn for sheeting, shirts and dresses more cheaply than homespun.

SMUGGLERS

Tench Coxe was a US Founding Father with a fascination for technology. He sent an English mechanic across the seas to England to make brass models of Arkwright's water frame spinner, but the models were seized and the mechanic forced to stay in England for three years.

The English, obsessively protective of the textile inventions, kept a close watch on exports, but that didn't prevent early industrial spies from trying to smuggle innovative machinery to America as cargo purposely mislabeled 'teeth for horse-rakes' (actually a shipment of spindles). ◆

Stephen Yafa, *Cotton: the biography of a revolutionary fiber*, Penguin 2005.

At the end of the 18th century not many clothes were made of cotton – around four per cent in England and the US combined. But just 100 years later nearly three-quarters of all clothing in the two countries was made from cotton. And part of the increase was due to more inventions, and more spying.

Eli Whitney was always tinkering about with things; he set up a nail factory when he was 14 years old. Later, while visiting a cotton plantation in Georgia, he met local farmers who complained about the difficulties of separating the Upland cotton fibers from the seeds. Each bale (roughly 500 pounds in weight) took up to 16 months of a slave's work to separate, and of course the slave had to be fed and clothed, which reduced profits. A few days later, Whitney had invented a form of gin to do the work mechanically – and at last the supply of cotton could meet the demand. It was boom time, and Cotton was King.

More money for the plantation owners, unfortunately, tended to mean increased misery for the slaves.

King Cotton

Why the increase in supply came from the US rather than India or China can be debated. The US had slavery, of course. But workers in the other two countries labored under conditions of near-slavery. In China, the Imperial yoke bore down on them. It was hard for peasants to take risks, and they had little time or money to play around with. There was also considerable anti-Western sentiment. The same is true in India; the British would

---

'Without slavery there would be no cotton, without cotton there would be no modern industry. It is slavery which has given value to the colonies, it is the colonies which have created world trade...'

Karl Marx

---

not allow mechanization and powerful, often absentee, local rulers would have creamed off any profits. The US benefited from the coincidence of capital and slavery.

Although fewer than 500,000 Africans were brought to North America during the slave trade, the slave population there grew to four million by the 1860 census. In 1850, there were 384,884 slave-owning cotton growers, and in Natchez, Mississippi, there were more millionaires per capita than anywhere else in the world. The wealth gave rise to the extravagant 'ante-bellum' houses with their wide verandahs, columns, heavy furniture and over-decorated interiors.

Life on the plantations fills many books, and there are some searing slave accounts of their cotton-picking days. The work was difficult at the best of times: the crop had to be picked at a certain time when weather conditions and ripeness concurred. In the steamy South, this was

SLAVE STORY

Charles Ball, born in the 1780s, worked on a 500-acre cotton plantation near Charleston, South Carolina. In addition to tending cotton, slaves grew corn, rice, indigo, sweet potatoes and peaches. They also made baskets and brooms, repaired farm equipment and had their own garden patches which they could tend on Sundays. The swampy land nearby was home to mosquitoes.

'The business of picking cotton constitutes about half the year's labor. It starts in September. The cotton being planted in hills, in straight rows, four to five feet apart, each hand or picker, provided with a bag holding a bushel or more hung round the neck, proceeds from one side of the field to the other picking all the cotton from the open burs. The cotton is gathered into the bag. A day's work is estimated by the pounds of cotton in the seed that the picker brings into the cotton house at night. In a good field fully ripe a day's work is 60 pounds; but where the cotton is inferior or the burs are not in full blow, 50, 40 or even 30 is as much as one hand can get in a day.

On all estates the standard of a day's work is fixed by the

back-breaking work, stooping over the shrubs to pick the bolls all day in hot sun. 'Planters knew that where cotton thrived, humans suffered,' writes social economist Pietra Rivoli. The toil was hard enough, but the sticky swampy heat of the Mississippi Delta – so perfect for cotton – was also home to snakes, bugs and vicious insects.

overseer, according to the quality of the cotton; and if a hand gathers more than this standard, he is paid for it; but if when his or her cotton is weighed at the cotton-house in the evening it is found that the standard quantity has not been picked, the delinquent picker is sure to receive a whipping.' ◆

From 'The Life and Adventures of Charles Ball' in
I was born a slave: an anthology of classic slave narratives,
ed Yuval Taylor, Payback Press/Canongate 1999.

From the outset, slavery in the US met with opposition, especially from the Quakers. In the first half of the 19th century, the abolition movement gathered momentum. The North, opposing slavery, and the Southern states that supported it grew apart and in 1845 their positions hardened when the Southern Baptists declared that it was acceptable for Christians to own slaves. The American Civil War (1861-1865) brought an end to formal slavery, but many freed slaves had nothing and soon became ensnared in another form of servitude as sharecroppers.

During the War, US cotton production fell: in 1860 it had been supplying 84 per cent of Britain's cotton but just two years later it provided only 7 per cent, and prices soared. Cotton from India – 'dirty, brittle and unpopular' – was rushed in, but many Lancashire mills fell silent and some 500,000 workers were destitute.

In America's Deep South, the bales of cotton began to pile up again, but the profits did not stack up. The post-War reconstruction period did not provide a leg-up for the cotton economy, and farmers were loath to try anything else. The textile mills had all been located in the North, but now investors saw an opportunity to build some in the South and these sucked both black and white poor people into their maws.

US raw cotton was still shipped to Britain, which by 1880 was exporting 80 per cent of its cotton goods to developing countries. But the US's new mills were modern while England's were old. It was an opportunity for the South to become the new hub, and in time the mills were producing high-class textiles... such as Levi's blue jeans with their unique rivets, patented in 1874.

Things were looking up for US cotton. But a little bug was waiting in the wings, licking its lips or rather waving its snout at the thought of all that cotton.

'All god's dangers ain't a white man'

Around 1892, a small creature made the crossing from Mexico to Texas, and was soon burrowing its snout into the cotton flower buds ('squares') or into the bolls across the southern states. The eggs soon hatched and hungry larvae ate whatever they were upon, destroying the plants. Nate Shaw, a black sharecropper in the early 20th century, wrote about his experiences in his book, *All God's Dangers*. And the danger that time round was not the white man, but the boll-weevil.

Before long, the voracious feeder had decimated yields; one farm managed just over 300 bales whereas pre-weevil it had produced nearly 14,000. All the might of US inventiveness and chemical concoction was brought to bear. But, as Stephen Yafa put it: 'The boll-weevil served to remind us that the forces of nature can lay waste the most ambitious designs of man [sic]. In the time it took to conquer this tiny bug, America had abandoned horses for automobiles, invented the airplane, fought in two world wars, developed the nuclear bomb, reached Mars and the moon, created computer and satellite technology, and learned to replace human heart valves with artificial ventricular assist pumps.'

Despite the weevil-wrought destruction, the US South continued to supply cotton to 75 per cent of the world's mills, and three-quarters of the world's population were clothed in something cotton. India supplied only 11 per cent, and Egypt about half that.

Nonetheless the pesky bug needed to be put in its place. But – like the mosquito – it proved very resistant to the waves of insecticides that were dusted, sprayed and washed over it. In the end, a combination of pesticide and bio-control has brought it under control. Meanwhile cotton growers looked to Washington for help, so setting in motion the support and subsidy system that is entrenched today, and helps ensure the US's position as one of the major producers of cotton, providing 20 per cent of world supply.

Birth of the blues

One good thing to emerge from the dire time of the boll-weevil's first ravages was the blues, which emerged directly from slavery and from the cotton fields. The gang-leader

BB AND THE BLUES

Born in 1925, Riley – later 'BB' – King grew up in a sharecropper's cabin and as a boy listened to his great-grandmother, a former slave, as she talked about the birth of the blues. Singing, she said, mattered just as much as breathing. In time, he heard the music of blues singers Lonnie Johnson and Blind Lemon Jefferson and he was entranced. He eventually got a guitar and began to play. The music he played and sang stood for everything; it saved his life.

Like other black Southerners who lived and worked on plantations, King was deeply attached to cotton: 'In the Mississippi Delta cotton was a force of nature. Like the sun and the moon and the stars above, it surrounded my life and invaded my dreams. I saw it, felt it, dealt with it every day. In a thousand ways I actually loved it. It was beautiful to live through the seasons... there's poetry to it, a feeling that I belonged and mattered. Hoeing and growing cotton has a steady rhythm, it's a study in patience and perseverance.' ◆

Stephen Yafa, *Cotton: the biography of a revolutionary fiber*, Penguin 2005.

sang the call-line, and the slaves responded. This rhythmical 'call and response' helped with the repetitive tasks and later evolved into the blues. The havoc caused by the boll-weevil found its way into the songs like 'Boll-weevil blues'. And so, as often happens, what brought disaster to one group brought a kind of salvation to others. The boll-weevil destroyed livelihoods, but the blues gave an opportunity, a way out of the cotton fields and a future to oppressed black people.

The rest of the world

Success for US cotton spelled the demise of other countries' cotton industries. After American independence in 1776, Britain's East India Company looked to 'improve' India's local varieties – that is, make them amenable to machine production. 'This benefited the Company and the English textile manufacturers, neither of whom cared about preserving Indian textile traditions, or the welfare of Indian farmers or weavers,' explains Uzramma of the Dastkar Andhra Trust, which supports the handloom industry. 'In fact they saw the Indian weaver as a competitor for the supply of cotton and the Indian farmer as inefficient, because he was unwilling to fit into the new trade-dominated industrial pattern.'

'Native Indian varieties were grown without irrigation on rain-fed soils, intercropped with the local food crops,' explains Uzramma. They fruited over a long period, and so could be picked by family labor. In other words, they

INDIAN COTTON

Cotton in India is grown largely by small farmers, and the new practices have changed the nature of farm practices from sustainable family-based agriculture to  intensive commercial farming with severe and tragic consequences. Seeds come from large multinationals rather than the farmer's own stock, and are expensive. While the local varieties were rain-fed, the new varieties need irrigation, which increases humidity. Humidity in turn encourages pests and fungus. A cocktail of chemicals – fertilizer, pesticide and fungicide – is used, which adds to the cost of cultivation but does not guarantee a good harvest. The farmer runs up huge debts hoping for a good crop, but India's weather is variable, groundwater is fast depleting and if the crop fails the risks are entirely the farmer's. The distress of the cotton farmer leads to numbers of suicides: in 2004, in the state of Andhra Pradesh alone, almost 600 farmers, the majority of them cotton growers, ended their lives. Lately the introduction of genetically modified seeds has led to even more severe problems in cotton-growing areas of Maharashtra and Andhra Pradesh. ◆

Uzramma of the Dastkar Andhra Trust, India.

were suited to 'an economy of dispersed rather than mass production. The new British machines on the other hand were the heralds of the era of mass-production, and they needed uniform raw materials in large quantities, and the need to grow cotton to supply those machines rather than for the local textile industry completely transformed cotton cultivation in India.'

After India regained its independence in 1947, mass production was synonymous with modernity and India's

---

CHINESE T-SHIRT

They called it 'bra wars'– but bras were only part of it. When the Multi-Fiber Arrangement (MFA) expired in January 2005, clothes made in China flooded into Europe and the US. In some instances EU imports rose by 500 per cent. Panic ensued, then customs hold-ups, followed by negotiations with China to limit textile imports in the next few years.

China may be flooding markets but it only receives a small portion of the profits from its textile exports. The value added is often as low as 10 per cent. The lion's share goes to Western corporations such as Wal-Mart and other brand companies sourcing products in China.

In fact, China's producers are in a bit of a fix thanks to their government. While negotiating accession to the WTO, China agreed that other countries could apply 'safeguard

---

own spinning and weaving mills took over the role of Lancashire in the textile industry. 'It was taken for granted that research into cotton varieties would continue to develop cotton for the mills,' comments Uzramma, 'making sure that the cotton plant kept pace with the development of the machines. American cotton varieties and their hybrids gradually replaced the native ones, so that at present the native varieties grow only in a few places.'

measures' to protect them from import surges from China. But domestically it played down these concessions and in 2004 producers went on a shopping spree for expensive foreign machinery to boost capacity.

When the US and EU re-imposed import barriers in mid-2005 Chinese producers were taken by surprise. Feeling the pressure are textile workers for whom a 15-hour working day is not unusual. Many are low-paid migrants from the countryside, brought in to replace more experienced (and expensive) workers. In Guangdong Province alone two million skilled workers were fired.

'Instead of viewing Chinese workers as competition,' says Chinese academic Dale Wen, 'labor movements outside of China should unite internationally and support Chinese workers' rights.' ◆

China

China's cotton-growing goes back a long way and by the 15th century, a textile industry flourished in the Yangtse region, with weaving done by people in the towns and the countryside. Over the next couple of centuries other, non-cotton-growing areas began to process cotton into cloth too. In the late 19th century, machine-spun yarn from Britain and India began to be used, and in the 1930s mechanized weaving came in, beginning to replace hand-looms. But China's consumption of cotton continued to rise, so the hand-looms were still busy. Under the Communists, the textile industry was reformed with nearly all cloth produced by power looms. Today China grows the most cotton in the world, and also imports cotton cloth to make into clothes for export – jeans and T-shirts for example.

3 Cultural icon

Since T-shirts made their appearance in US politics and film they have remained center stage, while cotton itself has often furnished a context or background setting: think of the 1936 Margaret Mitchell book and 1939 Hollywood film *Gone with the Wind*, which was set on a Georgia cotton plantation in the Civil War period. The idyllic view of the ante-bellum South, with its well-organized plantations, cheerful slaves and benevolent masters was only one side. In 1852, publication of *Uncle Tom's Cabin*, written by teacher and abolitionist Harriet Beecher Stowe, caused a storm. It focused on slavery and some felt that it was a trigger for the Civil War.

French impressionist painter Edgar Degas found him-

135,000 SETS. 270,000 VOLUMES SOLD.

UNCLE TOM'S CABIN

FOR SALE HERE.

AN EDITION FOR THE MILLION, COMPLETE IN 1 Vol., PRICE 37 1/2 CENTS.
"   "   IN GERMAN, IN 1 Vol., PRICE 50 CENTS.
"   "   IN 2 Vols., CLOTH, 6 PLATES, PRICE $1.50.
SUPERB ILLUSTRATED EDITION, IN 1 Vol., WITH 153 ENGRAVINGS.
PRICES FROM $2.50 TO $5.00.

The Greatest Book of the Age

UNCLE TOM

Uncle Tom's Cabin was the best-selling novel of the 19th century. In the first year after it was published, 300,000 copies of the book were sold in the US alone.

The book is credited with helping to fuel the abolitionist cause in the 1850s. Its impact was so great that when Abraham Lincoln met Stowe at the start of the American Civil War, Lincoln is often quoted as having declared, 'So this is the little lady who made this big war.'

The book has been criticized for its stereotyping of black people, and also for the character of Uncle Tom, the dutiful, long-suffering servant faithful to his white master or mistress. This characterization gave rise to the expression 'Uncle Tom' – a pejorative term for an African-American who is perceived by others as behaving in a subservient manner to white authority figures, or as seeking ingratiation with them. ◆

self in New Orleans in the 1870s when he was staying with relatives who were engaged in the cotton trade. On a visit to the Cotton Exchange, Degas observed people at their work. His resultant painting *The Cotton Exchange in New Orleans* (1873) shows the cotton traders absorbed as they pore over a bale of cotton opened out on the table, and the inspector or 'classer' seated in the foreground closely observing a skein of raw cotton. At that time, about one-third of America's cotton passed through New Orleans.

As mentioned earlier, working the cotton fields gave rise to a new song form, the blues. While picking the cotton, or hoeing the weeds out, the slaves would respond in unison to a call from the gang-leader (also a slave). Slaves used these call-and-response work songs and field 'hollers' (solitary shouts from one laborer to another or to the water carriers) to help set the pace, pass the time, and cope with the physical and mental stress of slavery in the cotton fields.

One of the most famous of these songs is *Pick a Bale of Cotton*. The Leadbelly version is the classic, but it was also recorded by many other artists from Harry Belafonte to Pete Seeger and Lonnie Donegan. Then there is Huddie Ledbetter's *Cotton Fields Back Home* – another sung by Leadbelly, but also recorded by, among others, Creedence Clearwater Revival and also by the Beach Boys, who gave it their distinctive surf sound treatment. Other cotton songs are *Old King Cotton*, *Cotton-eyed Joe*, and even military band composer John Sousa got in on the act with

The Cotton Club was a famous night club in New York City that operated during and after Prohibition. While the club featured many of the greatest African American entertainers of the era, such as Duke Ellington, Louis Armstrong and Ethel Waters, it generally denied admission to blacks. During its heyday, it served as a chic meeting spot in the heart of Harlem, featuring regular 'Celebrity Nights' with guests including Jimmy Durante, George Gershwin, Al Jolson, Mae West and Irving Berlin.

THE COTTON CLUB

It opened as the Club Deluxe in Harlem in 1920. Bootlegger and gangster Owney Madden took over the club in 1923 (while imprisoned in Sing Sing) and changed its name to the Cotton Club. It reproduced the racist imagery of the times, often depicting blacks as 'savages' in exotic jungles or as 'darkies' in the plantation South. Paul Robeson performed there after he graduated from Columbia Law School in 1923.

his *King Cotton March* (Sousa also wrote *The Stars and Stripes Forever*). And perhaps the most famous, Jerome Kern and Oscar Hammerstein's *Ol' Man River*, with its lines 'Tote dat barge/Lift dat bale.'

After the end of the Civil War, freed slaves moved north

Duke Ellington's orchestra was the house band there from 1927 to 1931. Ellington gained national exposure through radio broadcasts, and was able to develop his repertoire while composing not only the dance tunes for the shows, but also overtures, transitions, accompaniments, and 'jungle' effects that gave him the freedom to experiment with orchestral colors and arrangements that touring bands rarely had. Ellington recorded over 100 compositions during this era, while building the group that he led for nearly 50 years. The club eventually relaxed its policy of excluding black customers in deference to Ellington's request.

The Club closed in 1936 after the race riot in Harlem the previous year. It did reopen but closed for good in 1940, under pressure from higher rents, changing tastes and a federal investigation into tax evasion by Manhattan nightclub owners. The Cotton Club was reborn in 1978 in Harlem and today there are offshoot Cotton Clubs in the US and overseas.

The Cotton Club is also a movie directed by Francis Ford Coppola in 1984, which offers a fictionalized history of the club in the context of race relations in the 1930s. ◆

over time – and the music went with them. Many famous blues and jazz musicians, such as Duke Ellington, had their roots in the cotton plantations of the South and the way of life there – including picking the plants and the devastation caused by the boll-weevil – passed into

COTTON SONGS

Jump down, turn around
To pick a bale of cotton
Jump down, turn around
To pick a bale a day.

From *Pick a bale of cotton*

Don't you remember, don't you know,
Don't you remember Cotton-eyed Joe?
Cotton-eyed Joe, Cotton-eyed Joe,
What did make you treat me so?
I'd 'a' been married forty year ago
Ef it had n't a-been for Cotton-eyed Joe!

From *Cotton-eyed Joe*

the songs. In 1940, Ellington recorded the classic *Cotton Tail*. According to *All About Jazz* columnist David Rickert, this was an 'artistic triumph that would point to the direction jazz would take in the future and helped shape a new role... [it] didn't have to be music for jazz dancing, it could exist for its own sake.' This rich seam of music-making influenced many other forms, including hip-hop, which began in the New York of the 1970s. And hip-hop brings us back to T-shirts – you can't get away from them.

When I was a little bitty baby
My mama would rock me in the cradle,
In them old cotton fields back home.

From *Cotton fields back home*

You an' me, we sweat and strain
Body all achin' an' racked wid pain
Tote dat barge, lift dat bale
Git a little drunk, an' you lands in jail.
Ah gits weary an' sick of tryin'
Ah'm tired of livin' an' skeered of dyin'
But Ol'Man River
He jes' keeps rollin' along.

From *Ol' man river*

T-shirt style

As noted, T-shirts had their beginnings in war-time wear in the First World War and later, worn under the uniforms of the US army and navy. So were they lined up with the establishment? Well, not completely. From time to time, the subversive vest peeked out from under the jacket and played a role in rebellion. Marlon Brando's Johnny Strabler in the 1953 film, *The Wild One*, became a style icon with his leather jacket over a T-shirt –remember the poster of Brando leaning on his motorbike and staring out with intent? A couple of years later, in *Rebel Without a Cause*, James Dean's white T-shirt and moody slouch made him a classic anti-hero that kids could identify with. Then along came Elvis with his sexy moves and raising a storm. The T-shirt was claimed by the counter-culture, liberated from the nice boy crew-cut image.

As the T-shirt became an item of clothing in its own right, the potential for messages was seized upon. Political slogans, adverts, identity statements, publicity for artists, films, bands and brands – the T-shirt was the ideal billboard. Walt Disney was one of the earliest to get in there, with Mickey Mouse, while US colleges also saw the potential to advertise their sports teams. Business saw an opportunity in transforming a plain T-shirt that sold for $3 into a fashion statement that sold for $20. Soon everyone found a way to sell a T-shirt and make some money, at rock concerts, holiday resorts, movie theaters as well as in shopping malls.

But T-shirts are in some ways a classic 'street' item, picking up on new trends, reflecting the world around them – graffiti, cartoons, art styles, causes, jokes and in-your-face slogans.

MAKING IMAGES

Decorating T-shirts has evolved from simple dyeing and hand-painting. In the 1960s, artists emerged from their work for T-shirts and cover designs for record albums.

Screen-printing, invented over 4,000 years ago in China, has been a mainstay method of getting an image onto cloth. Cloth is stretched onto a frame. A stencil of the design is photographically created on the fabric, and then special inks are pushed through the stencil with a rubber blade.

Today, thermal printing takes just a few minutes. The graphic/image is printed from a computer onto thermal paper. Then, under high temperature and pressure, the graphic on paper is transferred onto the material. This instant process gives a high-resolution image with half-tones and ideally suits the individual markets. Today there are many websites offering a design and print T-shirt service where you can upload your own images or text.

Threadless.com invites designers to submit ideas to the site; viewers can then vote on the designs and the most popular go into production. ◆

T-shirts took off in the 1960s as the counter-culture developed and there was plenty to proclaim and protest about. Tie-dying shirts with psychedelic colors was easy and popular, while silk-screen printing gave voice to all kinds of anti-establishment slogans from the Vietnam War to legalizing drugs: 'Make love, not war' was a popular one. The stunning Alexander Korda image of Che Guevara is an all-time great; it is still popular as a T-shirt image 40 years after Che was killed.

Che was not the only fallen idol to be resurrected onto a T-shirt: among many others there were Bob Marley, Jimi Hendrix, Marilyn Monroe and John Lennon. Music has

---

THE WAR ON T-SHIRTS

In August 2005 Cindy Sheehan, the mother of a fallen soldier in Iraq, spent 26 days camped near President George W Bush's ranch in Crawford, Texas as a protest. In January 2006 Bush was embarrassed by the publicity around her arrest in the Capitol building, just before his State of the Union address. Police Sergeant Kimberly Schneider said Sheehan had been arrested and taken in handcuffs to police headquarters because she had worn a T-shirt that showed the number of soldiers killed in Iraq: '2,245 Dead. How many more?' ◆

---

always been big on T-shirts, from images of The Beatles to commemorative rock concert ones, to the big red tongue stretching out from lascivious lips synonymous with Mick Jagger and the Rolling Stones.

Work by pop artists like Andy Warhol and Roy Liechtenstein also found its way onto T-shirts, as did that of cartoonists and graffitists. Warhol's famous depiction of Marilyn Monroe's face must have launched at least a thousand T-shirts.

Protest and survive

On the political front, 'Bush is the Terrorist' and 'Beware Blair' were two popular anti-Iraq war slogans. Some protestors at the WTO meeting in Cancún in 2003 had T-shirts that stated baldly 'Capitalism is Death'.

British designer Katherine Hamnett became in/famous for her protest T-shirts. In 1984 she famously wore an anti-nuclear T-shirt proclaiming '58% Don't Want Pershing' when she went to Downing Street to meet Margaret Thatcher. But she did not stop there: in 2003 models went down the catwalk in London wearing Hamnett T-shirts bearing 'No War, Blair Out'. Hamnett has also called for action on pollution and for cancellation of Third World debt. She used London Fashion Week – and model Naomi Campbell – to urge people living in HIV/AIDS-ravaged Africa to wear condoms. According to the BBC's Anna Browning, Hamnett's T-shirts are 'copyable', because she liked the idea of the copiers unwittingly promoting her messages. But she recognizes the limitations of T-shirt power, pointing to the vast march before the invasion of Iraq, when thousands wore anti-war T-shirts but the Government took no notice. She understands

---

T-SHIRT

When You're Not Here (I Sleep In Your T-Shirt)

I Wish You Were Here (To Take Off Your T-Shirt)

After We Make Love (I Sleep In Your T-Shirt)

Wake Up In Your T-Shirt,

Still Smell The Scent Of Your Cologne

When I Need Your Feel (I Sleep In Your T-Shirt)

I Need Help (To Take Off Your T-Shirt)

After We Make Love (I Sleep In Your T-Shirt)

Wake Up In Your T-Shirt,

Still Smell The Scent Of Your Cologne

Destiny's Child

---

the danger with T-shirts (and marches) that they 'give people the feeling that they have done something when they haven't'.

New designs

New designers are coming up with new ideas all the time; some good, and some, like Spamshirt... yes, you guessed it. Why just look at ***SPAM*** on a computer screen when you could be wearing that T-shirt saying 'Be the 9-inch man your goddess craves' or 'Buy cheap Viagra through us'.

While in Australia, ex-con turned comedian Mark Brandon Read, aka Chopper, had T-shirts created from his criminal past, including his fingerprint, rap sheet and police record photos.

Cotton threads its way into just about every art form, almost without our noticing. Beautiful fabrics, the canvas used for paintings, inspiration for blues singers, spur to invention, and ubiquitous item of clothing, not least the T-shirt which is the subject of the 2004 song by Destiny's Child.

But the T-shirt, along with other textiles and goods, is a source of grief in the workplace and at hotly contested trade negotiations. All is not fair in trade.

4 Free trade to fair trade

When pulling on a favorite T-shirt, we probably don't think too much about where or how it was made. The label may well say 'China' or 'Bangladesh' but the cotton itself may have been grown in Texas which now grows more cotton than any other US state.

Today, cotton is grown in 80 countries around the world from the US to Egypt and Brazil to China. In 2006/7 world production was 117 million bales (a bale weighs 480 pounds or 13 metric tons) – the second largest crop on record. The area of land growing cotton stood at about 35 million hectares or three per cent less than the previous year. But as for consumption, well, we love the stuff and cannot get enough of it: a new record was set in 2006/7

AFRICAN T-SHIRT

Moussa Faye lives in Senegal. 'When I was a child all my school uniform, all my clothes were made in Senegal. Now we have almost no textile industry left.'

The African cotton garment is rapidly becoming a thing of past – and with it goes an important industrial sector in the world's least industrialized continent. Cheap imports from richer countries (where cotton production is heavily subsidized) have decimated local production. US subsidies have enabled American cotton to be exported at up to 40 per cent less than it cost to produce.

In a landmark ruling, the WTO upheld a complaint from Brazil, backed by a number of African countries, about US subsidies. After much wrangling, US negotiators at the Hong Kong summit finally gave a 2007 date for ending export subsidies. This was a high-profile, but piffling gesture. Only a fraction of the $4 billion

of over 120 million bales. As recently as 2000/1 production was just under 100 million bales and consumption 94 million, so the growth is marked.

China produces the most cotton with around 30 million bales, followed by the US with 22 million and India around the 20 million mark. But cotton is also a significant crop in many other countries such as Pakistan, Brazil, Burkina Faso, Senegal and Turkey as well as in

Souvenir Senegal football T-shirt, probably made in China.

a year given to US cotton producers takes the form of 'export' subsidies anyway; most are classed as domestic.

Besides, the richer countries now have a more important target in sight – access to non-agricultural markets (NAMA) in the South. This will require developing countries to slash import tariffs, with serious consequences for local employment. 'In Senegal more than 30 per cent of industrial jobs have already gone because of tariff disarmament,' says Moussa Faye. 'Tariffs are the only instrument left to protect or rebuild our industry. I think that Europe and the US are preparing a new colonization. They need markets and are targeting the middle classes who have purchasing power in emerging countries.' ◆

several of the Central Asian 'stans' like Uzbekistan. And many of the poorer countries are bound in to the production of T-shirts, jeans and other cotton goods for export to the malls and high streets of the West.

As we've seen, cotton is big business. And the US is in the forefront of controlling trade to its advantage. While proclaiming themselves in favor of a level playing field, richer countries in fact distort trade by subsidizing their own producers, who then dump their agricultural goods on world markets at prices way below what it would cost anyone to produce them. This bolsters farming in the EU and North America, but hammers poor countries by flooding their markets and undercutting local producers. 'Most of the stupendous $4-billion-a-year cotton

'KEEP BUYING BANGLADESHI TEXTILES'

Textiles are Bangladesh's number one business. Two to three million Bangladeshis work in the industry and 85 per cent of them are women. Garments account for 76 per cent of the country's export earnings – no other country is so reliant on just one manufactured export. Such a heavy reliance makes Bangladesh extremely vulnerable to the vagaries of world trade. This poor and densely populated country is living, in every sense of the word, on the edge. The workers have quotas to fill. They are making children's and sports leisure wear for the German label Shamp, which in Europe sells shorts for the equivalent of 50 cents a piece, leggings for $1.50. This factory works with fabrics largely imported from China.

Like many others, it survives by selling experienced, plentiful labor – very cheap. The word both owners and workers hate to hear is 'China'. Buyers are quick to point out that Chinese suppliers can fulfill orders much more quickly. 'But Chinese workers have no right to speak out at all!' exclaims labor rights activist Nazma Akter. She says that health and safety conditions subsidies the US has been dishing out went to just 25,000 producers, of whom 8,000 were agribusiness corporations,' notes *New Internationalist* editor Vanessa Baird. Majority World consumers don't benefit either. 'What is the point of a cheaper pair of jeans if they have cost you your job? To get a sense of scale, US cotton subsidies

in Bangladesh's factories have improved considerably in recent years as a direct result of pressure from NGOs, consumers and campaign groups, such as No Sweat, Maquila Solidarity Network, Clean Clothes Campaign, Labour Behind the Label and others.

Today, the Bangladeshi companies with direct contracts with the well-known foreign chains (especially ones that have been campaigned against) tend to have the best conditions; the worst are the sub-contractors. The message going out to bosses is that 'compliance' with codes such as the Ethical Trading Initiative and ILO standards is key to gaining the better contracts. Now the NGOs must insist on an ethical price too.

If you find yourself wondering how that new T-shirt – made in Bangladesh – was so amazingly cheap, the answer is right here. So what's the answer? You might be tempted to avoid cheap Bangladeshi goods.

'No!' yells Nazma. 'Keep buying!'

'Keep buying!' says the factory owner, Lutfor Rahman. 'And tell your NGO and human rights people to defend Bangladeshi jobs!' ◆

alone have put in jeopardy the livelihoods of 10 million African farmers.

World Trade Organization

The World Trade Organization, dominated by rich world agendas, preaches the free trade doctrine. Few organizations are hated with such passion all around the world. Anger directed at the World Trade Organization and its activities spilled out most memorably on to the streets of Seattle in 1999 and Cancún in 2003.

The WTO is accused of causing hunger: forcing migration; ruining environments; denying poor people life-saving drugs; destroying health services and putting essential utilities like water out of the reach of the poor; even killing farmers. Through its intervention, jobs disappear, wages are depressed, people suffer poverty and abuses of human rights; biodiversity is threatened and fish-stocks depleted... the charge list goes on. So what exactly is this organization?

Born in 1995, it emerged from an earlier system, the General Agreement on Tariffs and Trade (GATT). Since 1948 this had presided over a succession of international trade negotiations focusing mainly on tariffs and quotas.

The main function of the WTO is to ensure that

member governments keep their trade policies within agreed limits. Once signed, the agreements provide the legal ground rules for international trade within a multilateral framework. According to the agreement that set up the WTO, its purpose is to facilitate trade and foster the sustainable long-term economic development and improvement of living standards in rich and poor countries alike.

One of its core principles is that national rules should not discriminate between a country's trading partners but grant all of them equally 'most favored nation' status. A country cannot favor its own products and must give foreign suppliers and companies exactly the same treatment. Another key principle is that trade should become progressively 'freer', with a lowering of trade barriers over time through negotiations. And trade arrangements should be predictable so that foreign companies, investors and governments can be confident that trade barriers will not be raised arbitrarily.

Interestingly, given the actions of rich countries in recent years, another principle is that the WTO should discourage 'unfair' practices such as export subsidies and dumping products at below their cost of production to gain market share.

Last, but by no means least, rules should be more beneficial for less developed countries, giving them more time
to adjust, greater flexibility and special privileges.

That's the theory. Critics, including most aid agencies, say
that on balance the WTO has done little that could be described as 'beneficial' to developing countries. Instead it has
presided over a system that has forced open poor world markets to the advantage of the rich world and its corporations.
The result has been deepening poverty and inequality.

The organization exerts extraordinary power in a
world where international trade agreements can override
not only national economic policies but even multilateral
agreements that relate to labor, human rights or environmental protection.

Defenders of the WTO argue that it is a membership
organization which can only do what its members – now
comprising 149 national governments – agree. It is also
more democratic than many international bodies as it operates on a one member one vote system. On the face of it, this
is so. But that does not mean its procedures are democratic,
transparent or fair. At the Hong Kong Ministerial meeting
Margaret Ateng Otim, a trade delegate and MP from Ugan-
da, said: 'It's like George Orwell's *Animal Farm*. All animals
are equal, but some are more equal than others.'

GATS and NAMA

Today, the fastest-growing area of global trade is through GATS (General Agreement on Trade in Services) by which markets in water, electricity, banking and healthcare are opened up by rich world corporations via the WTO.

And for Majority World textile workers, there is the specter of NAMA (Non-Agricultural Market Access) whereby developing countries are pressured to cut import duties, and open up their markets to predatory companies from the rich world. Shamina Nasrin, a worker in Bangladesh, explains that, if it is implemented, 'The women garment workers will be the worst sufferers. We will lose our textile industries. It is not favorable to us. We will lose jobs. We want to keep our own industries.'

Fair trade

Fair trade is an incredible story. When it emerged, four decades ago, few could have imagined it would ever be more than a form of charity, aimed at a dedicated few – not an idea that could ever reach a mass market.

Today one in five cups of coffee drunk in Britain is fairly traded; so are half the

INDIA'S 'POWERLOOM PRISON'

India's textile industry is not dying – it is still the single largest industry, comprising a fifth of the country's industrial production. But it has changed irrevocably.

Mumbai was once India's largest textile center, but now not a single mill operates here. What happened to the city's 250,000 workers? 'Most can't find work, and have moved back to their village. Some are working in temporary jobs as taxi drivers or security guards,' says Datta Ishwalkar from the Girni Kamgar Sangharsh Samiti (Mill Workers Struggle Association).

As work shifted from the composite mills in Mumbai to powerloom sweatshops in Bhiwandi (outside Mumbai) and other smaller cities, so did some workers. The composite mills were large, regulated and mostly unionized workplaces where there were machines to spin the yarn, weave it into cloth on looms and then process it. All processes took place in one location. In Bhiwandi, the yarn is bought and then spun into cloth and then sent for processing elsewhere. There is no regulation, taxes

bananas eaten in Switzerland. Five million producers in Africa, Latin America and Asia benefit from fair trade terms. In the West it's the fastest growing retail area – expanding by 20-30 per cent a year since 2000.

Still, reservations exist – with reason. It remains a drop in the ocean of world trade; it is caricatured as a niche and duties are avoided, labor is much cheaper and conditions are medieval. Cotton farmers aren't the only ones living in poverty. Powerloom workers and handloom weavers are barely managing to survive. Dire deprivation extends right down the cotton chain.

Sharad Panda moved to Bhiwandi when the composite mill he worked at in Mumbai shut up shop. He earned a third more five years ago in Mumbai than he earns now. 'In Mumbai, I got 4,500 rupees ($95.74) per month to work two looms for eight hours, plus a bonus of 8,000 rupees ($170.21) and leave. Here, I work four looms and earn 3,000 rupees ($63.83), with no security or leave,' says Sharad. 'It's not enough to support my family. The owners don't pay wages on time. Sometimes I have to borrow to make ends meet. I can't save anything to send my parents in the village. I could support them when I worked in the mill.' ◆

From 'Powerloom prison' by Dionne Bunsha in
New Internationalist No 399 www.newint.org

market for middle-class consumers in rich countries. And recently the thorny issue of certification – that is, who can use the 'Fair Trade' mark – has provoked fierce controversy.

Blushes rose and hearts fell when the Fairtrade Foundation in Britain gave the mark to Nestlé – a transnational notorious both for its dismal labor record in the South and its persistently irresponsible marketing of babymilk to people who do not have clean water to prepare it, or money to keep buying sufficient quantities.

Briefly, those standards are that fair traders should: support the poorest producers; deal fairly and openly with trading partners; develop the skills of producers and create opportunities for trading; and ensure that producers get a fair price.

They should also: inform customers as to where their goods came from; provide equal pay and opportunities for women and men; and ensure that producers are working in a healthy and safe place. Finally, they should not exploit child labor and they should make sure that the materials used in production and packaging do not damage the environment.

But for others fair trade presents a far more radical challenge. According to Wolfgang Sachs of the Wuppertal Institute: 'Fair trade is a thorn in the flesh of the established trading system.'

'The WTO looks at the world as a conflict among nations or groups of nations,' Sachs continues, explaining that fair trade has a different paradigm. 'It highlights that maybe market access at borders is the wrong focus, national regulations are not what is distorting trade... The power of the transnational corporations governing global markets is a much more distorting factor than differences between countries.'

There are other fundamental differences. 'The WTO is about cheap prices. The welfare of the consumer is at the center of this regime. With fair trade the producer is at the center of attention; you start from there.'

And you have to start with a fair price. 'A fair price can only be a full cost price,' says Sachs. 'Prices are not fair if they do not tell the truth. The present system is one that systematically tells lies.'

Also, because it takes account of the producer, fair trade can address the issue of poverty directly, rather than through the questionable assumption that economic growth will automatically alleviate poverty. The Fair Trade Federation in the US estimates that small farmers get up to 40 per cent more by selling through fair trade.

China

'Free trade is working for big business tycoons but it's a failure for workers,' says LC Yan of the Hong Kong Confederation of Trades Unions. 'Workers are suffering from free trade policies and we are unable to protect them. Wages are five to ten times higher in Hong Kong than in China, but the cost of living is more than ten times higher.'

Lucky workers in mainland China, you might conclude. Hong Kong's loss is their gain. It's a story that is repeated and reported in newspapers in many parts of the world. Or, in the words of Mexico's former President Vicente Fox, the Chinese are 'stealing' Mexican jobs.

It may come as a surprise, then, to learn that China's trade miracle has done almost nothing to increase em-

---

ETHICAL T-SHIRT

Welcome to the fair trade T-shirt, coming to a store near you. Perhaps. While some of the big chains are looking to develop their own 'fair trade' line of clothing, many consumers have been dressing ethically for some time now, buying fair trade and organic clothes from the websites of a growing number of alternative clothing companies.

Fair trade initiatives are helping small-scale cotton growers in India, Mali, Senegal and Peru to get a decent price for their product. If the cotton is organic, too, then the benefits are doubled. Currently cotton accounts for a tenth of all pesticides and more than a fifth of all insecticides used in agriculture. This poisons not only the environment but farmers too. The Pesticides Action Network reports that 20,000 people in the developing

---

ployment in the country. While the 1990s saw China's economy growing at an astonishing 10.4 per cent a year, net employment growth was as low as 1.1 per cent.

Nanotechnology

And there are new clouds on the horizon. These include developments such as the use of nanotechnology in cotton textiles. Nanotechnology is the science of manipulating things at the molecular level, where key components are measured in nanometers, or one-billionth of a meter. A

world die each year from agricultural pesticides; three million suffer acute or reproductive after-effects. However, there are some serious limitations to the new fair trade cotton mark recently launched by the London-based Fairtrade Foundation. It applies only to the production and purchase of the raw cotton, not to the subsequent spinning, weaving or making of clothes.

But don't despair – some of the better alternative clothes retailers do follow the product line right through. People Tree, for example, uses organic cotton grown in India which is made up into clothes by a fair trade project for deaf women.

Meanwhile there are moves elsewhere to introduce a 'social label' on clothing, which would certify that human rights and International Labor Organization core labor standards have been observed during production. ◆

GRANDMOTHER'S SARI

It is the year 2035, and Asha is thinking about her grandmother's cotton sari. It seemed to Asha that each time cotton production and so-called 'technological progress' joined hands it was the poor who lost out. For example, the shift in textile production to England and cultivation by slaves in the American South led to mass starvation in India, where cotton was still hand-picked and hand-woven. Not only were the Indian weavers contending with the factory system but the British also imposed harsh restrictions on the export of India's finished cloth to protect their new industrialists. Rebellious weavers who attempted to evade these restrictions had their fingers smashed by the muskets of British soldiers. In a cruel twist of history, the rifles used to exact this punishment were of a type invented and patented by cotton-gin inventor Eli Whitney.

When the father of Indian independence, Mahatma Gandhi, talked about giving power back to the poor, he drew a direct link between technology, politics and cotton. 'I think of the

Reuters report noted that nanotechnology applications now being developed 'range from the fantastic – a supercomputer small enough to fit in your hand – to the mundane: stain-resistant khakis and longer-lasting tennis balls'. Probably the most visible nanotech products to poor of India every time that I draw a thread on the wheel,' he said, urging India to turn away from mechanized production and return to hand-spinning of cotton to revitalize its village economies. Mechanization of spinning, he claimed, 'brought on slavery, pauperism and disappearance of the inimitable artistic talent which was once all expressed in the wonderful fabric of India which was the envy of the world.'

When Asha put on the sari she discovered that it was unexpectedly soft to wear. She liked how the breeze went through it, but mostly she liked the way its colors faded. The new nano-fabrics didn't do that. They stayed clean and shiny perpetually. Like so many new technologies, they existed in an unsullied present with no stain of history. That felt wrong to Asha – it dishonored the cotton weavers who'd had their fingers crushed by rifles, the American slaves who'd worked the plantations and the cotton families who'd lost their livelihood to nanofibers. When she was next scheduled to see her grandmother, Asha made a point of wearing the cotton sari. ◆

From 'Whatever happened to cotton?' by Jim Thomas in
New Internationalist No 399 www.newint.org

date are the stain- and wrinkle-resistant slacks developed by North Carolina-based Nano-Tex LLC and sold as Levi Dockers and Lee Jeans, amongst others. Billions of tiny whiskers create a thin cushion of air above the cotton fabric, smoothing out wrinkles and allowing liquids to bead up and roll off without a trace.

The whiskers are added by dipping cotton fabric in a proprietary chemical solution before the fabric is cut. Because the particles are so small, they easily penetrate the fabric and coat each cotton thread completely without changing the way it looks or feels.

The company has developed similar stain-resistant products for synthetic fibers and upholstery. One new product wraps synthetic fibers in an organic, cotton-like substance to create a garment that combines the longevity of polyester with the comfortable feel of natural fabric. Just like genetically modified cotton, or GM anything, people are anxious about what nanotechnology will really mean.

Food miles... fabric miles

Nanotechnology is one 'advance' and we are not sure where it will take us or the planet. We do know, however, that freighting goods around is definitely damaging our world. We're familiar with the idea of food miles – asparagus grown in Peru being jetted to supermarkets in England, for example, or garlic from China ending up in Canada. But of course the same happens with cotton goods. Cotton grown in the US may well go to India to be spun into yarn and then travel to China to be fashioned into T-shirts and other clothes, before being shipped back to the US or Europe for sale.

And if you think sea-freight is less damaging to the environment than air transport, the UK *Guardian* newspaper reported in March 2007 that shipping is responsible for 4-5 per cent of carbon emissions, compared with 2 per cent for aviation. The answer: use local produce, which would mean a lot less cotton garb for most of us. But then, what about the fair trade producers (and non-fair trade ones for that matter) in the South who rely on overseas purchasers of their tea, coffee and other commodities? In an ideal world, all trade would be fair and there would probably be less need to freight stuff – from iPods to T-shirts, from coffee to jeans – around the globe because we'd recognize that it is not sustainable to carry on as we are. But this would represent a major change for most people in the West, as we have come to expect everything to be in our shops all the time. Clothes are more than a way to keep warm: for some, they are a statement about who we are.

5 Brand new fashions

In the light of cotton's slave connections, 'branding' takes on additional meaning. But the purposes were the same. Branding was the practice of making a permanent mark of ownership, often with a hot iron. Slaves were branded with their owner's mark, and criminals used to be 'fixed with a mark of infamy'. In that way, branding signified somebody's fall from grace, or their subservient position.

The brand – a name, trademark or symbol like a logo – tells us where the item comes from, its provenance. In commerce, the brand is owned by the company who use it to distinguish their goods from other people's. Some have been so successful that their brand name has become a generic term for an item, as in 'my old Hoover' or 'my favorite Levi's' or 'a bowl of Kelloggs' for breakfast. And some are so generic that they have lost the capital letter, like thermos, aspirin or yo-yo.

So how did the idea of pushing a brand for consumer goods come about? 'It's a marketing given that the consumer defines the brand,' said Sir Michael Perry, head of Unilever. 'But the brand also defines the consumer. We are what we wear, what we eat, what we drive.'

Jane Pavitt in *brand.new* notes how shopping has been transformed from a mundane activity – as in 'doing the shopping' – to something pleasurable, self-gratifying, when we 'go shopping'. Pavitt adds, 'Selecting or rejecting brands can be part of the process of defining our lifestyles and of presenting an identity to the world.' What we purchase speaks for us.

But of course this does not just happen. We are manipulated by clever advertising and marketing, the use of celebrities, and a misjudged sense of freedom and individuality as we herd along the mall buying and wearing the same things as others in our 'clan'. We wear *these* jeans, whereas those are *sooo* lame, or just so Nineties.

Relatively obscure brands can become overnight fashion musts when a celebrity puts them on, as happened in 2003 when Justin Timberlake donned Von Dutch stuff, soon followed by Britney Spears and P Diddy.

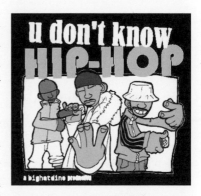

And hip-hop has developed its own fashion cool with the drop-down baggy jeans and big T-shirts. In his book on cotton, Stephen Yafa cites Damien Lemon, 25-year-old artist on *Vibe* magazine: 'The hip-hop consumer is, if not the most, then one of the most savvy customers in the game. We'll buy something impulsively if it's the hot new shit, but if it can't stand up to the quality or what we need it for – if it's not durable – it's going to fall off quick, you know what I mean? That's one of the thing that Akademiks [brand] is all dope with. Their quality is bananas while it's stylistically dope, too.' Guess he doesn't like that brand...

Behind what we purchase is a carefully constructed set of ideas and marketing mechanisms to deepen the emotional link between us the consumer and the goods we buy. The marketers want to make us identify with *their* brand, and work to make us feel special, and above all

HOW TO WEAR A T-SHIRT

Ever since Frankie said we should Relax, slogans on T-shirts have been popular. But they are a potential fashion disaster if you get the wrong one.

Rule 1 - No band T-shirts

Never wear a band T-shirt. Ever. For a start, it looks a bit sad. All those people mooching around in their nihilistic NIN long-sleeved tops, or with Marilyn Manson's face staring out at you, or, if you are of a certain age, Iron Maiden's Eddy reaching out towards you. It's tacky, don't bother. If you can't suggest the type of music you enjoy through your usual style of dress, then stay indoors.

Rule 2 - No logos

Don't pay to advertise Nike. Pay to advertise yourself. You are not your T-shirt brand. You are all individuals. Tell them to FCUK off.

Rule 3 - No drugs

Ok, I'm going to say this now, to get it out of the way. Drugs aren't cool. I'm not saying don't do drugs, because, well, drugs can be fun. But they are not fucking cool. Face it, who makes a big thing out of doing drugs.

It's not counter-culture or revolutionary to be proud of smoking dope. It's like walking round, acting tough because you smoke Silk Cut. Get a fucking life and a better T-shirt

Rule 4 - Retro

Rhoobarb. Pob. Dangermouse. Hartley Hare. Heroes and icons every one. I will not deny these shirts their time in the sun, just remember that today's Retro is tomorrow's nostalgia and next Wednesday's dork. If you buy one of these shirts, remember it has a short shelf-life.

Rule 5 - Political slogans

I remember I used to have a T-shirt of a young woman shouting at a soldier, who was doing his best to ignore her and not shoot her with the big fuck-off gun he was pointing just past her. It was a 'Get out of Ireland' T-shirt. While I wore it, where I lived was never, ever targeted by the IRA. Such is the power of political T-shirts. Either that or where I live is so boring even the IRA wouldn't bomb it.

Political T-shirts are great fun, you feel good wearing them, like you're really making a difference. Then someone starts an argument with you in a pub over it and, well, things get complicated and you wish you'd worn your Clangers one instead.

Rule 6 – 'Funny' T-shirts

Oh, how we laugh at those wonderful T-shirts advertised in *Fortean Times* or *Bizarre* and on t-shirthell.com. They are so funny. The first time. So while that slogan looks witty on the web site and puts an interesting spin on the Star Wars logo, ask yourself, after you've stood at an ironing board staring at it for the 17th time, is it still funny?

Obviously the thing to remember with anything is context. Wearing a T-shirt stating you're 'not a terrorist' on the Tube might not be the best idea. Most people won't get the joke. But wearing it to a party will make you the most popular person there.

The solution is to have either many slogan T-shirts, so you are never caught wearing the same one twice. Or just have a select handful, to be deployed strategically. ◆

From Deborah Taylor *Mookychick* www.mookychick.co.uk

loyal to that logo – even if the shoes or T-shirt are basically the same as every other brand, or even – perish the thought – as every other non-branded item...

Just swoosh it!

T-shirts, like jeans, epitomize the best and worst of the garment trade and the fashion industry. They are the normal, basic, cheap, comfy everyday item that everybody loves to wear. But they can

also be the purveyors of fashion and cool. It has to be the *right* T-shirt. For lots of people, that means the current cool brand, and for lots of people at one time that was Nike with its in/famous 'Swoosh' swirl, and slogan 'Just Do It'.

Nike, one of the biggest sportswear outfitters, has been the target of campaigners with its use of sweatshop labor in Mexico, Vietnam, Indonesia and China. 'No story illustrates the growing distrust of the culture of corporate branding more than the international anti-Nike movement,' says Naomi Klein, activist and author of *No Logo*. Despite protests, Nike's annual revenues have increased from $6.4 billion in 1996 to $15 billion in 2006. It maintains its high profile partly by sponsoring sports stars such as Maria Sharapova, LeBron James, Cristiano Ronaldo, Lance Armstrong, Kobe Bryant, Michael Jordan and Aaron Lennon. Nike has cleaned up its image in the US, but Boycott Nike alleges that it 'continues its goal to sabotage any labor organization that stands in its way.'

Beat them at their own game...
Global justice activists have found clever ways to subvert the power of brands, by mimicry, mockery and great humor. Adbusters' version of 'Marlborough Man' has him standing, a drooping cigarette hanging from his mouth, with the 'logo' in place behind him – except it says 'Impotent' instead of 'Marlborough'. Adbusters have done a range of spoof ads, many on fashion.

For example, their one featuring a group of sheep in front of a fence draped in the stars and stripes. In the bottom right corner is the Tommy Hilfiger logo with the strapline 'Follow the Flock'. And their take on 'The

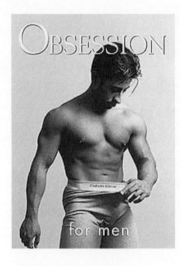

Colors of Benetton' shows an exec with greenbacks (dollars) stuffed in his mouth showing the power of money.

And who hasn't laughed at their anti-ad where, under the heading 'Obsession', the fit guy looks down anxiously... or admiringly perhaps... into his Calvin Klein boxers.

6 Tying up the ends

T-shirts are big business: the industry is currently worth around $60 billion a year. The challenge is to have more support for Majority World producers, on fair terms. Fair trade items are now increasingly on sale, including jeans and T-shirts. But a UK survey of under-25s found that 'more than half (58 per cent) do not care how their clothes are produced' and did not take notice of ethical issues such as whether child labor or sweatshops were involved, or damage to the environment. But Rachel Neame of ethical clothing company People Tree feels that younger people do care: People Tree's core market is the 25-40 age group. Let's hope she's right, for T-shirts are vital wear for that age group, even though many people don't keep their clothes for long. A report by Cambridge University in December 2006, called *Well dressed?* explained how 70 per cent of unwanted clothes in the UK are chucked out and end up in landfill sites. They are cheap to buy and therefore easily discarded. On the way, they may have been washed 65 times, tumble-dried and ironed – amounting to greater energy use than it took to produce the material and ship it.

On the throwaway topic, there is a whole industry built on shipping used clothes to developing countries. Until recently trade barriers were in place to protect markets such as in Africa. But now an organized industry buys clothes that are donated to charity shops or thrown away. And at the other end, in Tanzania for example, there is a similar network of traders sorting and selling the clothes in a lively and lucrative business. *Mitumba* is the name given to clothing thrown away by the West. Pietra Rivoli notes that 90 per cent of a clothes-bale's value comes from just 10 per cent of the clothes. 'For every GAP shirt in perfect condition that might fetch $3.00 there will be a dozen pieces that will be hard to unload even at 50 cents.' It's good to know that the clothes don't just go into landfill, but quite sad that they are so in demand. Sociologist Karen Hansen researched the *mitumba* market in

Zambia and found that its availability is seen as a sign of progress in villages – 'There is even *mitumba* now,' residents would say, indicating improved quality of life.

A major British chain store, Marks & Spencer is now producing some fair trade goods, with cotton supplied by

GOT THE T-SHIRT...
T-SHIRT SLOGANS

Apartheid Divides, UDM Unites
(South Africa, United Democratic Movement)

There is no Planet B

Ya Basta!
(EZLN – Zapatistas. Rough translation is 'Enough')

Fight War, not Wars

$ellout

I will not advertise your company on my T-shirt

Make Trade Fair
(Oxfam)

Relax

I'm Here, I'm Queer, Now Buy Me A Beer

My parents went to Peru/Las Vegas/The Moon and all I got was this lousy T-shirt

Be Kind to Animals – Don't Eat Them
(Vegetarian Society et al)

the Djdgan Cotton Farmers' Cooperative Union, a partnership of 36 village co-ops in Mali. The cotton is picked
in Mali, processed into fabric in Belgium, then shipped to
Morocco to be manufactured, labeled and finished. The
money from the cotton is invested in schools, teachers, a
well and a seed storage warehouse.

Going organic

Many people are moving into organic cotton, even in Texas. 'In west Texas alone, cotton causes 13.8 million pounds

---

T-SHIRT COSTS

Sam Maher of Look Behind the Label, which campaigns against
sweatshops, says: 'When you buy a T-shirt for a few pounds,
it's only so cheap because someone else is paying the cost.'

- Cotton (probably GM) grown and spun into yarn in US at
  $1.10 per shirt.
- Shipped to Asia for bleaching, dying and sewing: cost now
  $2.16.
- Made in a sweatshop – many women work up to 12 hours
  a day, 7 days a week. Each worker earns just 86 cents a day.
  The T-shirt costs $3.92 at this stage.
- Shipped to the West – finished garments at the wholesalers
  cost $5.30.
- Into the shops – profits abound: the T-shirt sells for $8-20. ◆

---

of agricultural pollutants to be dumped into the soil, water, and air every year,' says LaRhea Pepper. Since 1978, she and her husband have been farming 1,400 acres in northwest Texas. And for the past decade, the Peppers, along with 30 other cotton farmers in the area, have been championing organic cotton. In 2001, they banded together as the Texas Organic Cotton Marketing Cooperative, producing about 3,000 quarter-ton bales of cotton, making it the nation's leading supplier of truly natural cotton.

But there's a long way to go. Organics constitute less than one per cent of the cotton planted in the US, according to Helen Cordes of *Utne* magazine. And farmers need reliable customers to justify the risk in switching over to organic growing. Cotton Plus, the co-op's first business, which sells a wide variety of organic-cotton fabrics, hopes to boost the markets. 'If manufacturers and consumers demand our organic cotton, the ripple effect could turn into a tidal wave,' says LaRhea. 'We can bring our soil back to life, clean up the water, and return farmers to being the true stewards of the soil.'

In India, there is likewise a move into organic growing and also fair trade. Chetna Organic in Hyderabad, currently with 1,500 farmers, began in 2004 with financial backing from a Dutch development organization. It is

WHAT IS AN ORGANIC T-SHIRT?

• It is made from cotton that is grown organically.

• It does not contain chemicals.

• It promotes the development of wildlife.

• It respects the fertility of the soil.

• It is better quality than intensively farmed cotton.

• There are no artificial softeners.

• There are no bleaching agents. ◆

a certified fair trade project which benefits participating farmers. For example, Rajlakshmi Cotton Mills will source 70 per cent of its organic cotton in 2006-2007 from Chetna Organic. The project hopes to increase to 17,000 farmers by 2010 and produce 20 per cent of the organic cotton grown in India. Within a year or two, it is expected to become one of the largest organic and fair trade cotton projects in the world.

But will going organic help Indian and other farmers in the long run? In theory, of course it will. But it will take time: the soil may be depleted by years of chemicals. On top of this, there is a lot for farmers to learn and absorb about crop management once they no longer simply spray chemicals on it. Kavitha Kuruganti at Hyderabad's Center for Sustainable Agriculture explains: 'What civil society is doing is trying to swim against the tide.' And that means battling against the Government, the World Bank and other forces that only care about production totals. Kuruganti says that while organic is not alone sufficient to address the whole problem, it is essential for improved farmer livelihoods as well as for the environment. Organic 'needs to enter the mainstream, and a fair trade premium is welcome.'

In the meantime, we can use our T-shirts as an interesting way to look at the world – from issues about fashion and cool to brand-names and sponsorship, from Indian peasants to Chinese sweatshop workers, from hi-dose pesticides to organic cotton production. They may be a relatively new item of clothing, but T-shirts tell all the stories.

> 'The web of our life is of a mingled yarn, good and ill together.'
> *William Shakespeare*

CONTACTS

AUSTRALIA
Global Trade Watch www.tradewatchoz.org
Australian Fair Trade and Investment Network www.aftinet.org.au
Fair Trade Association of Australia and New Zealand www.fta.org.au
CANADA
Transfair Canada www.transfair.ca
BRITAIN
Trade Justice Movement www.tjm.org.uk
World Development Movement www.wdm.org.uk
Fairtrade Foundation www.fairtrade.org.uk
Pesticide Action Network www.pan-uk.org
No Sweat www.nosweat.org.uk
Labour Behind the Label www.labourbehindthelabel.org
IRELAND
Trade Justice Ireland www.tradejustice.ie
NEW ZEALAND/AOTEAROA
Trade Aid www.tradeaid.org.nz
Aotearoa/New Zealand Fair Trade Association www.fta.org.nz
Christian World Service www.cws.org.nz
Oxfam New Zealand www.oxfam.org.nz
UNITED STATES
Transfair USA www.transfairusa.org
US Interfaith Trade Justice Campaign info@tradejusticeusa.org
OTHER
Third World Network www.twnside.org.sg
Via Campesina International Farmers' Network www.viacampesina.org
The International Fair Trade Association (IFAT) www.ifat.org
International Confederation of Free Trade Unions www.icftu.org
Friends of the Earth International www.foei.org
Greenpeace International www.greenpeace.org/international_en/
Seattle to Brussels Network www.s2bnetwork.org

RESOURCES

Global Trade: Past Mistakes Future Choices by Greg Buckman, Zed 2005.
Behind the Scenes at the WTO by Fatoumata Jawara and Aileen Kwa, Zed Books/Focus on the Global South, 2003.
Trade Justice: Turning Words Into Action An excellent new campaign guide from Christian Aid. Available from email: info@christian-aid.org tel:+44 20 7523 2225
Trade Justice, *New Internationalist* Issue 388, April 2006 www.newint.org